My Ballet Comic Book

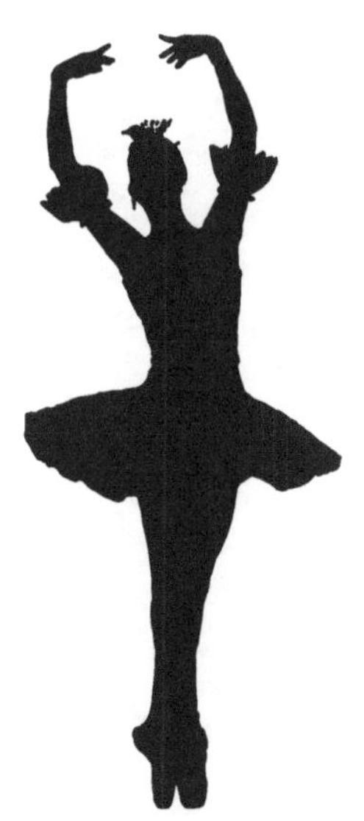

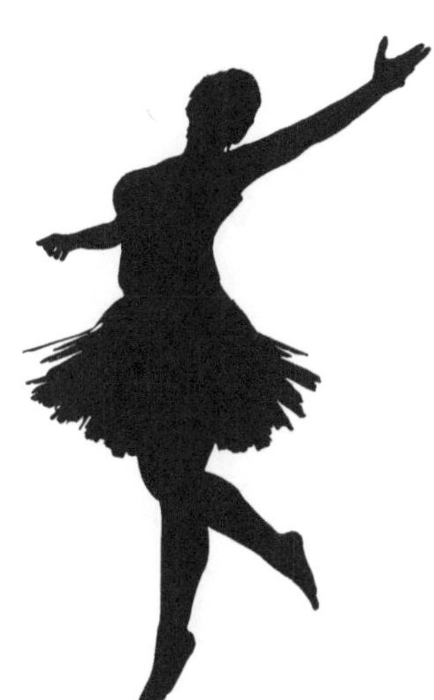

This Book Belongs To

. . . .

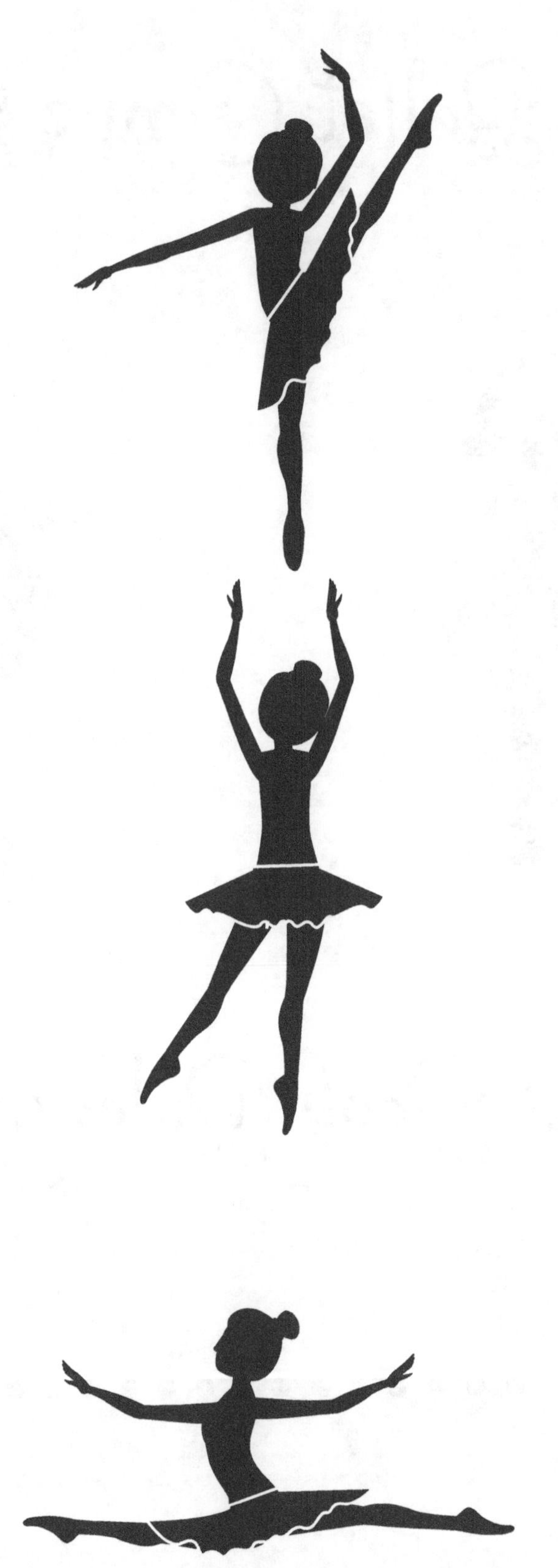

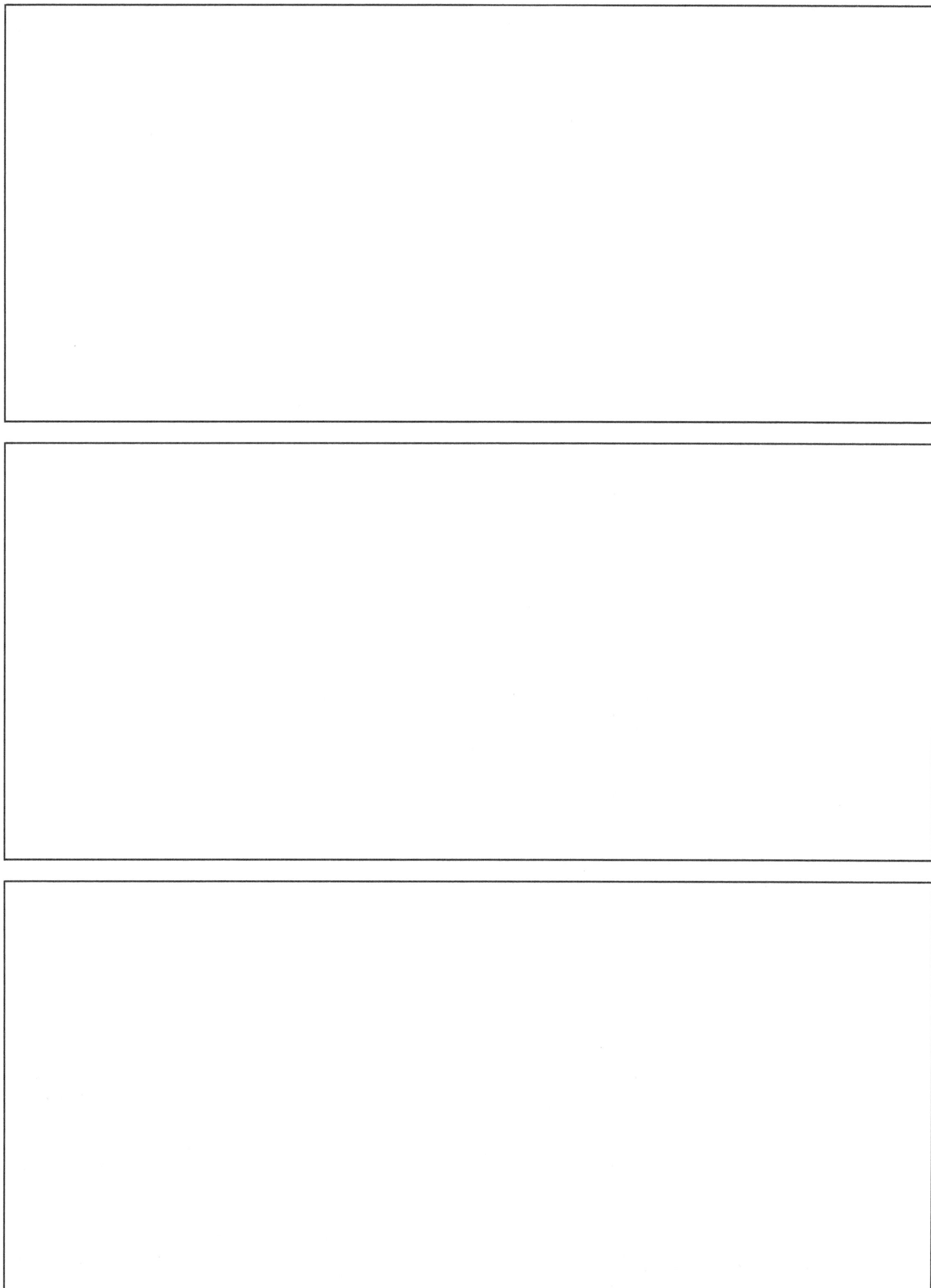

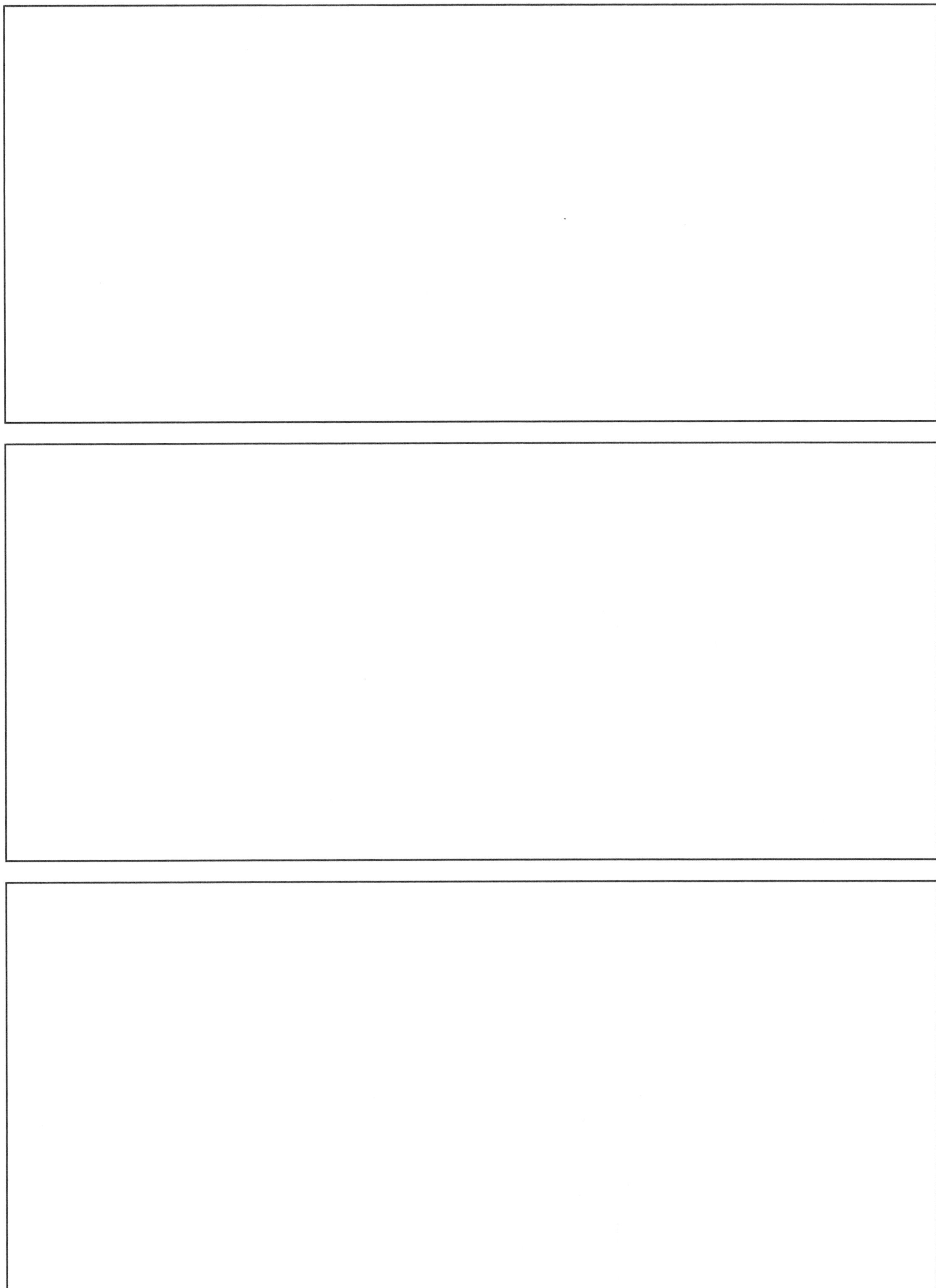

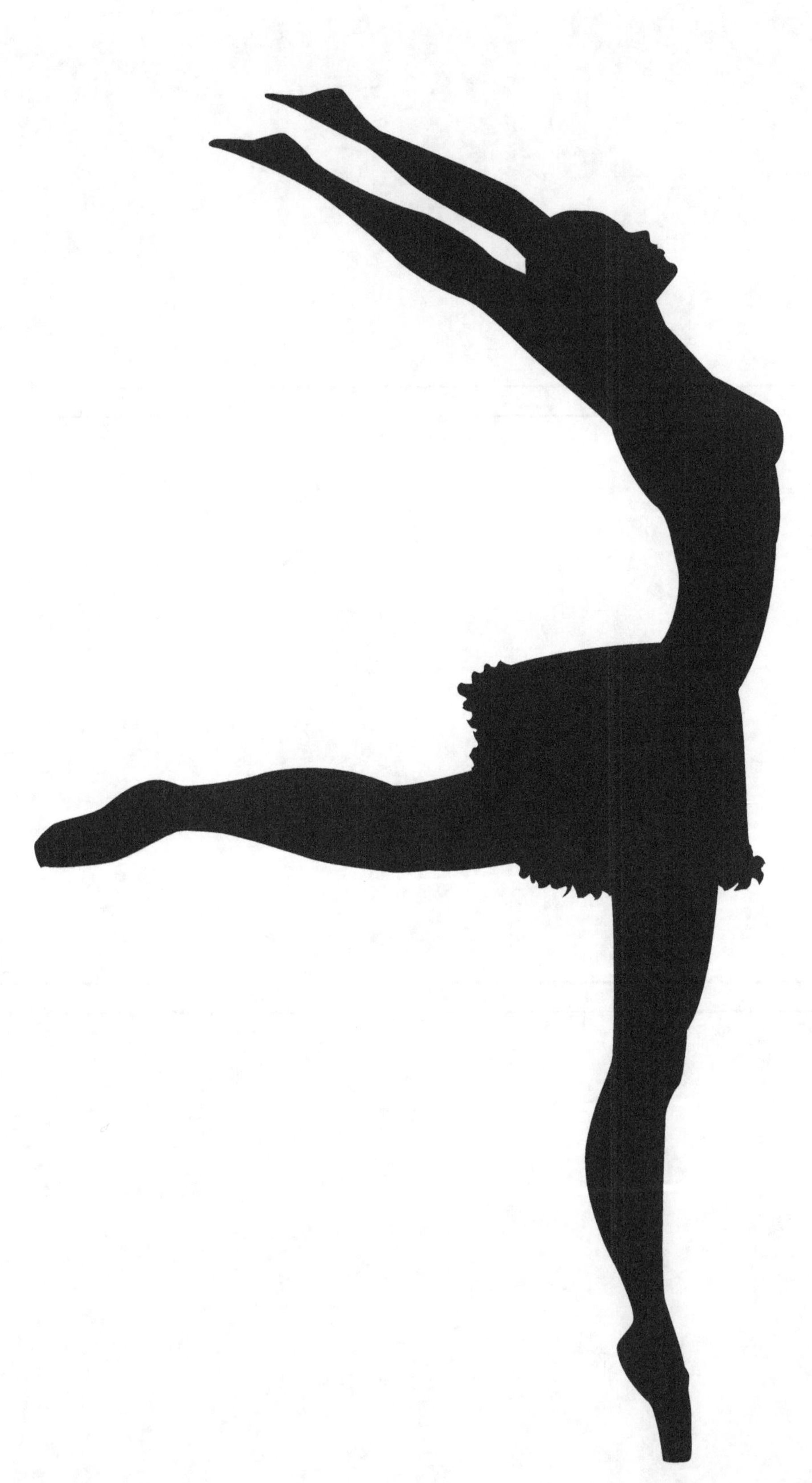

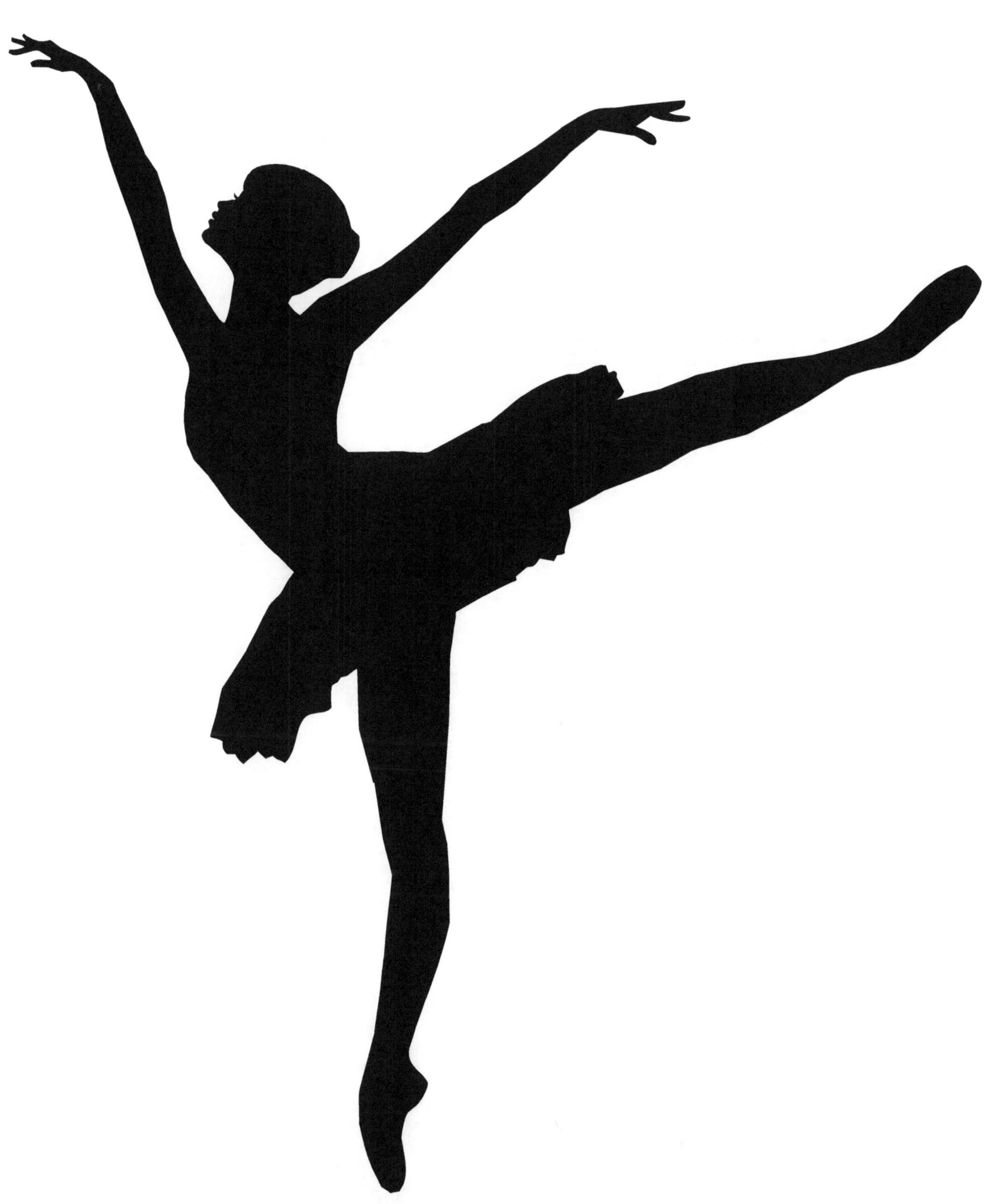

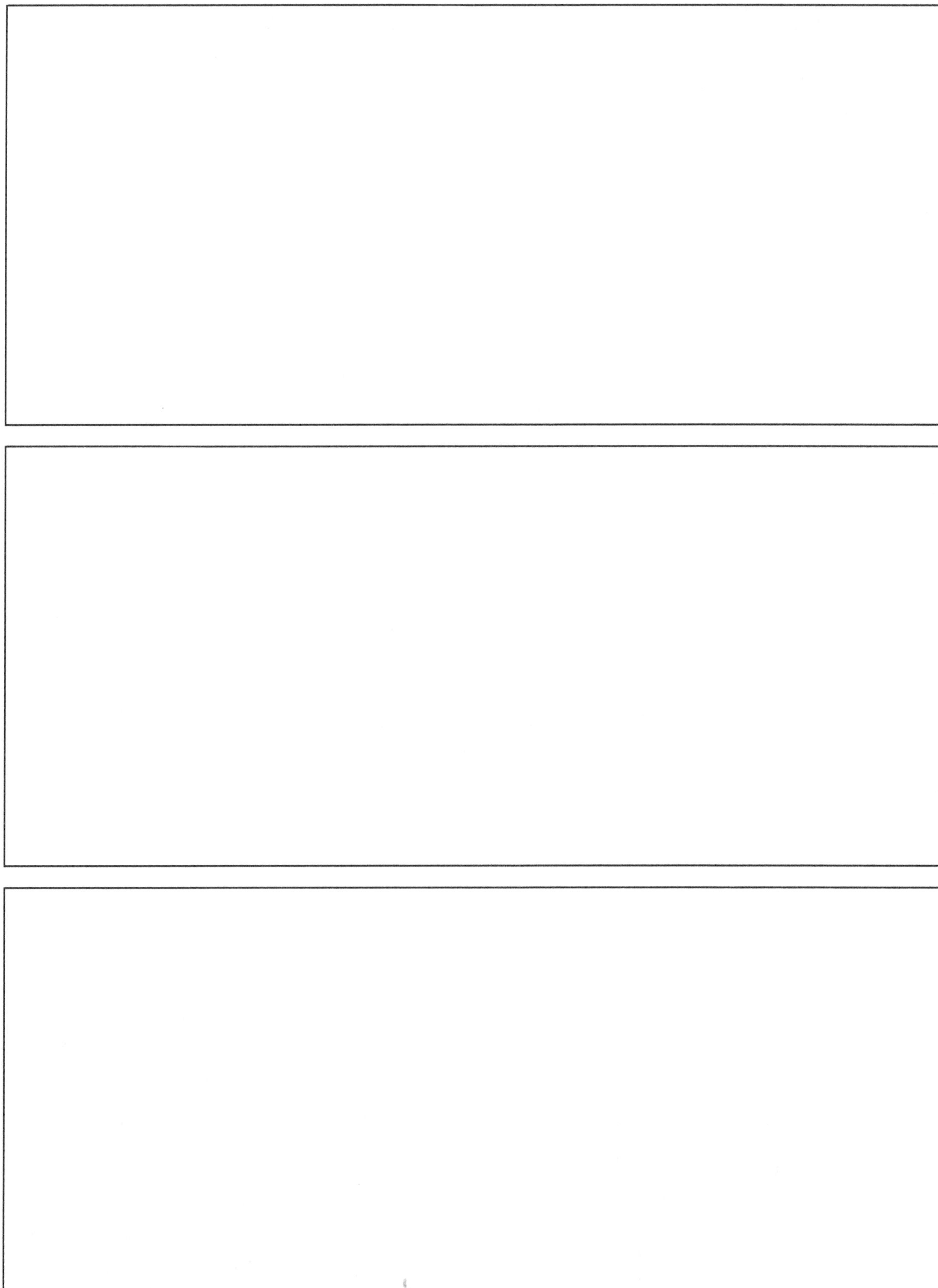

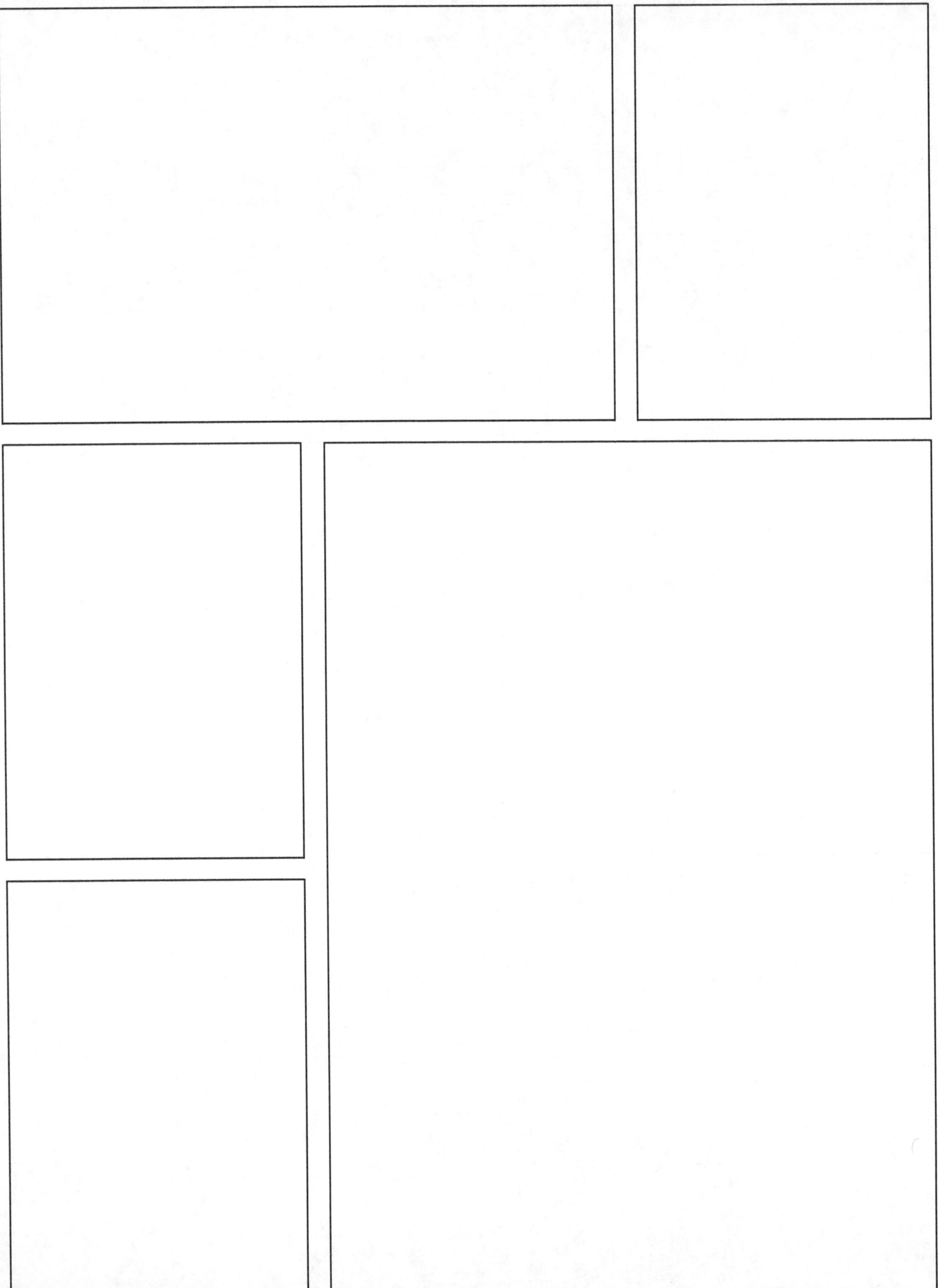

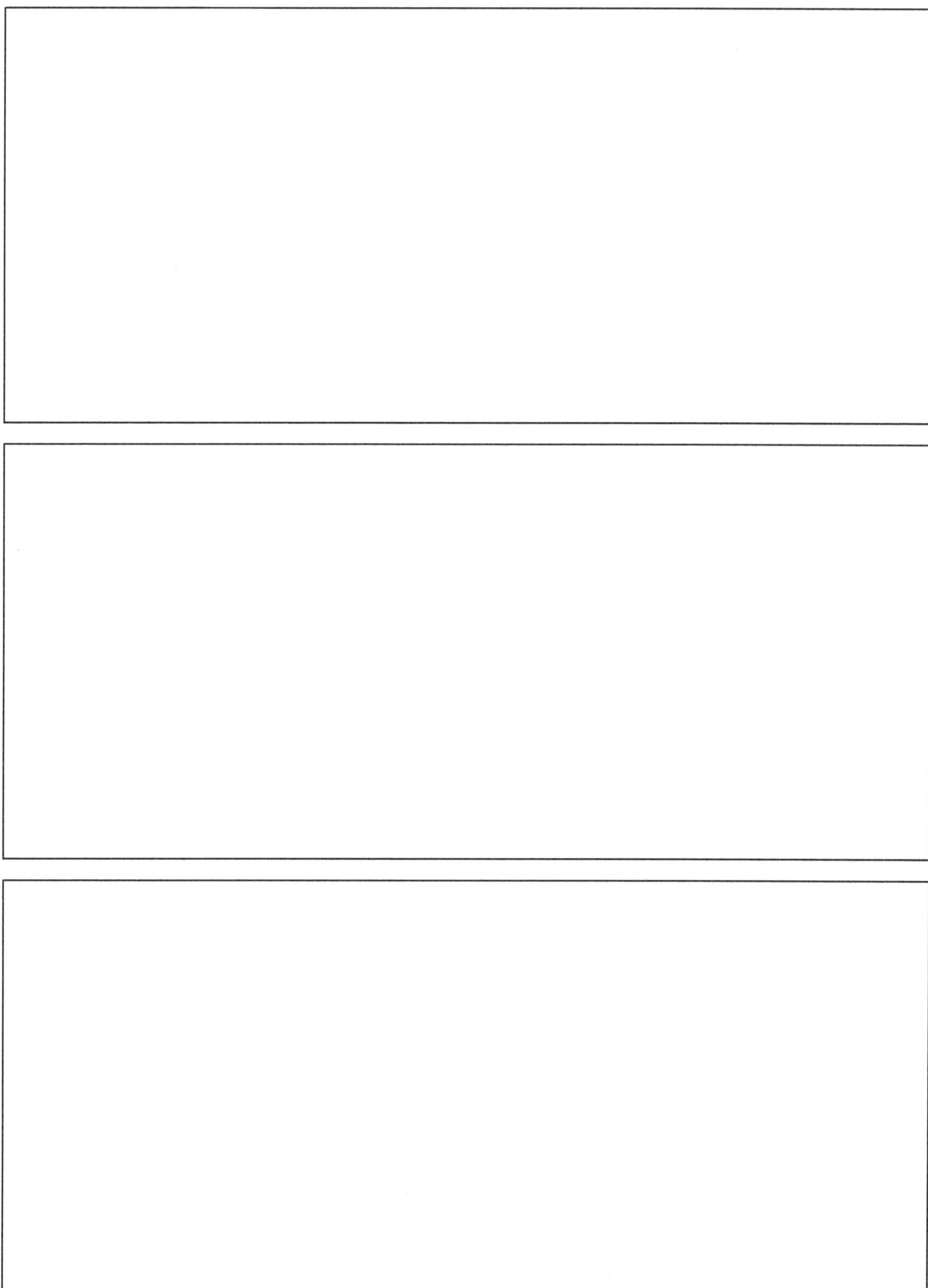

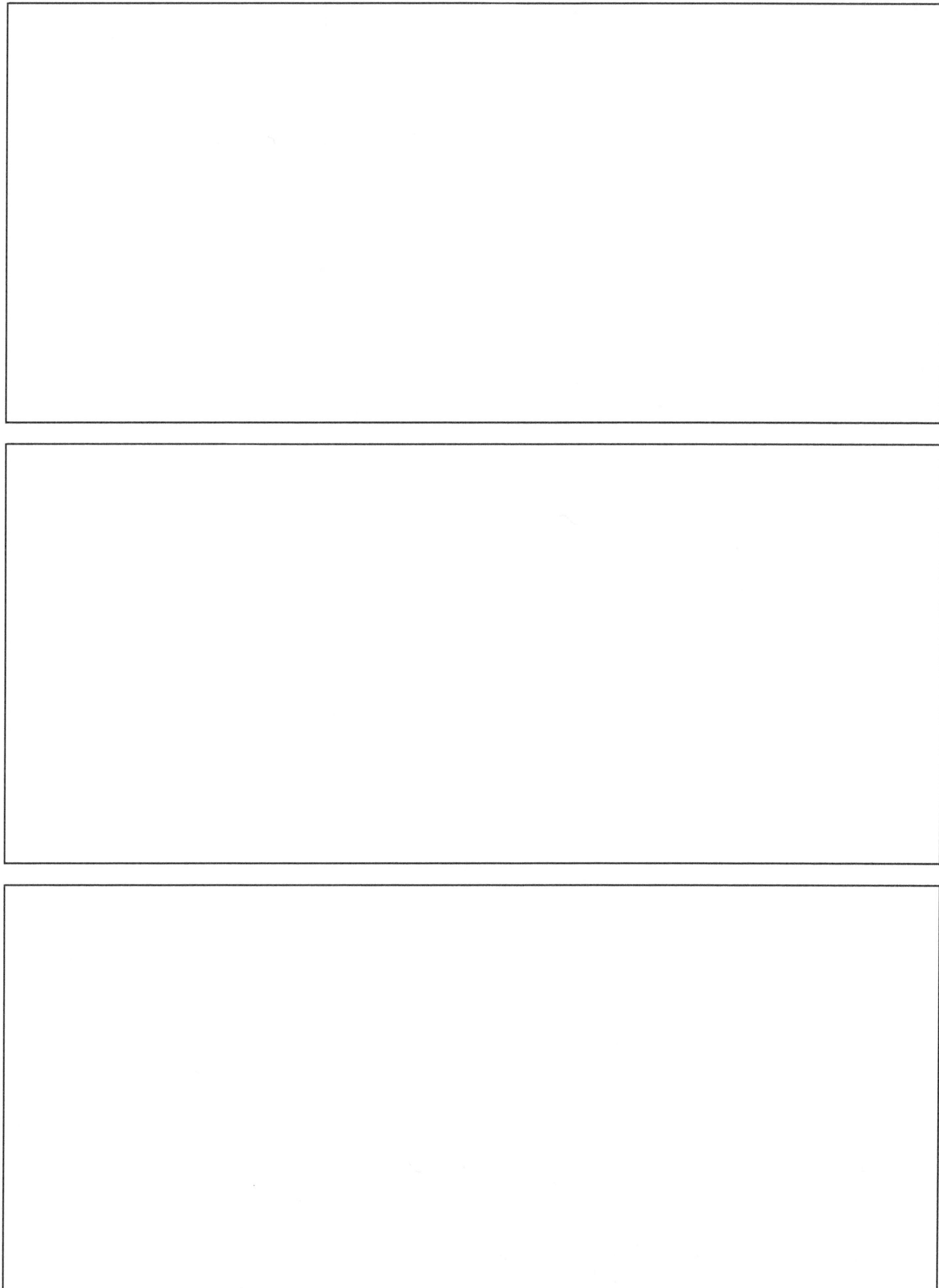

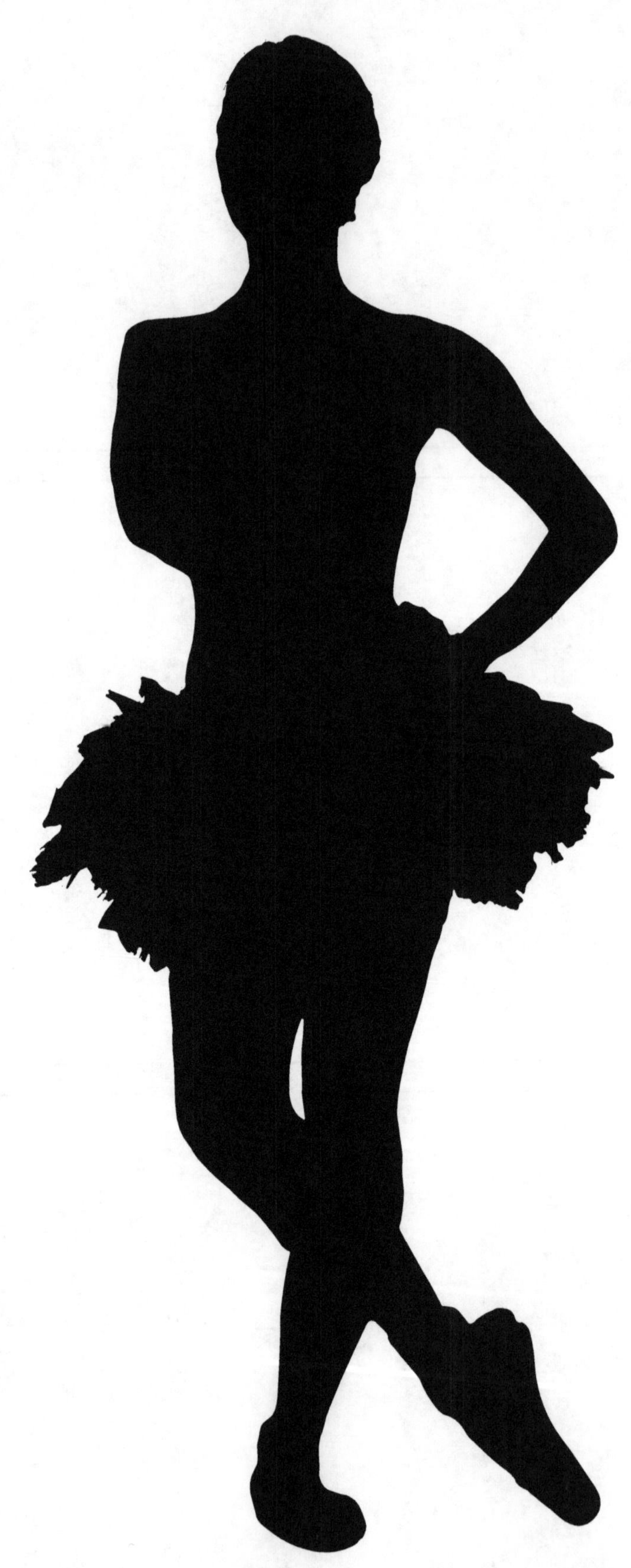